On My Own

Dear Parent,

   If you are considering whether or not to leave your child alone—either for an evening while you go to the movies or every day while you are at work—then *On My Own* will help both you and your child prepare for this new situation.

Lynette Long

The Kids' Self Care Book

On My Own

by Lynette Long, Ph.D.

illustrated by Jo Ann Hall

ACROPOLIS BOOKS LTD.

WASHINGTON, D.C.

Reprinted June 1984

ACROPOLIS BOOKS, LTD.
Colortone Building, 2400 17th Street, N.W.
Washington, D.C. 20009

Printed in the United States of America by
COLORTONE PRESS
Creative Graphics, Inc.
Washington, D.C. 20009

Attention: Schools and Corporations
ACROPOLIS books are available at quantity discounts with bulk purchase for educational, business, or sales promotional use. For further information, please write to: SPECIAL SALES DEPARTMENT, ACROPOLIS BOOKS, LTD., 2400 17th ST., N.W., WASHINGTON, D.C. 20009.

**Are there Acropolis Books you want
but cannot find in your local stores?**
You can get any Acropolis book title in print. Simply send title and retail price, plus 50 cents for postage and handling costs for each book desired. District of Columbia residents add applicable sales tax. Enclose check or money order only, no cash please, to: ACROPOLIS BOOKS LTD., 2400 17th ST., N.W., WASHINGTON, D.C. 20009.

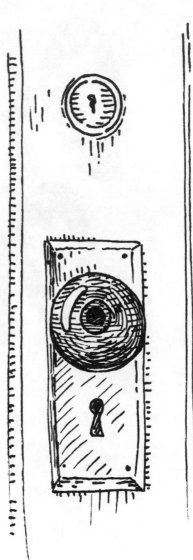

Library of Congress Cataloging Publication Data

Long, Lynette.
 On my own.

 Includes index.
 Summary: A guide for children of working parents which teaches self-care in such areas as getting ready for school, after school, using the telephone, snacks, outside and inside play, safety, emergencies, and fear.
 1. Latchkey children—Juvenile literature. 2. Children of woring parents—Juvenile literature. 3. Life skills—Juvenile literature. [1. Latchkey children. 2. Childen of working parents. 3. Life skills] I.Title.
HQ777.65.L67 1984.   640'.24054   84-463
ISBN 0-87491-735-2 (pbk.)

Table of Contents

Dear Parent,

If you are considering whether or not to leave your child alone—either for an evening while you go to the movies or every day while you are at work—then *On My Own* will help both you and your child prepare for this new situation.

There are at least 6.5 million children in the United States who take care of themselves while their parents work. Yet research has shown that many of them could be better prepared for the self-care experience. In fact, children who are not adequately prepared are much more vulnerable to physical and psychological risks.

As an educator and child psychologist I have discussed these potential problems with hundreds of children and adults. *On My Own* is the result. It is a workbook for eight to twelve-year-olds, designed to minimize the risks and to make staying alone a more positive, constructive experience.

Helping your children complete the more than 125 activities in this book, will definitely begin their preparation for taking care of themselves. They will learn how to handle emergencies, and actually minimize the chance of such emergencies occuring. They'll learn how to cope with fear and boredom, and even how to feel a greater sense of independence and security while you're away. At the same time, as a parent, you'll be more comfortable about leaving them alone.

Because circumstances and rules vary from family to family, many of the activities in this book ask the child to discuss situations with you, so that both of you know exactly what you expect of them. There are places to list the phone numbers you think are important, space to add rules you want followed, and charts to help you both organize the time they'll spend alone.

The last chapter is very important. It is a multiple choice quiz that asks your child to pick what she would do in certain situations that have actually happened to other children. The right choices and the reasons for those choices are given at the end of the quiz.

After your child has taken this quiz, you'll have a much better idea of whether or not he is ready for self-care. However, a child who scores high may not necessarily be ready. You must consider his maturity, the amount of time he will be expected to stay alone, the safety of your neighborhood and the availability of neighbors. And, when you do decide to leave your child unsupervised, please be cautious.

Sincerely,

Lynette Long

Lynette Long, Ph.D.

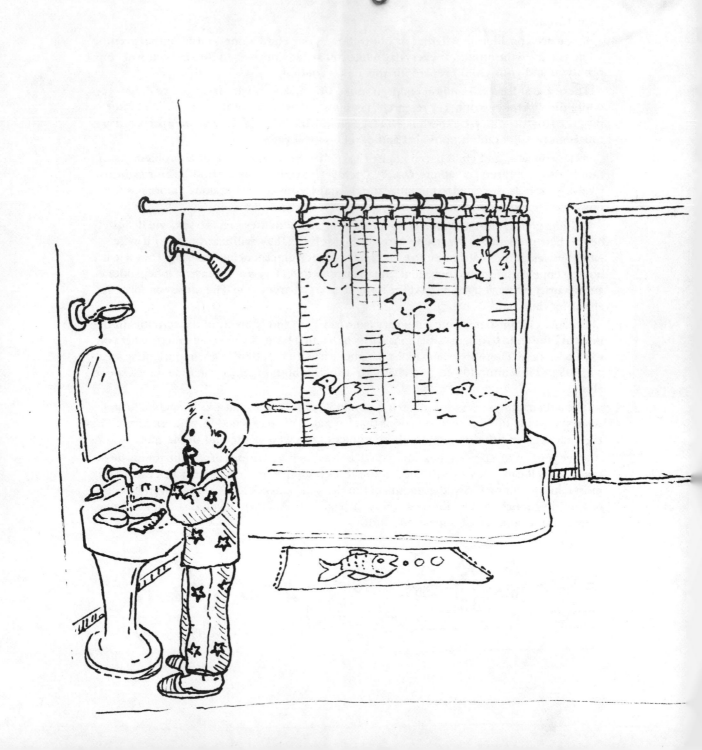

Chapter 1

Getting Ready For School

Morning is a very busy time. Parents are getting ready for work. Children are getting ready for school. This chapter will help make your mornings less rushed. It will teach you how to make breakfast and lunch. It will give your day a better start.

Times to Know

If you are alone in the morning, it is important to get ready and get to school on time.

Fill in the times you need to remember:

Wake up

_____

Leave for School

_____

Be at School

_____

Getting Ready For School

Bathroom Checklist

It is important to go to school clean. Before you leave in the morning, wash your face and hands, brush your teeth, and comb your hair. Here is a chart that will help you keep track of your bathroom activities for one week. Put a STAR in each box after you do each thing.

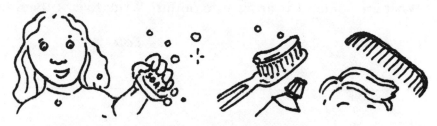

	Washed Face	Washed Hands	Brushed Teeth	Combed Hair
Monday				
Tuesday				
Wednesday				
Thursday				
Friday				

Matching Clothes

Choose your clothes for the next day before going to bed. Pick a top (shirt or blouse) and a bottom (pants or skirt) that go well together.

What are some of your favorite outfits? Write five of them here.

Bottom	*Top*
1. _____	_____
2. _____	_____
3. _____	_____
4. _____	_____
5. _____	_____

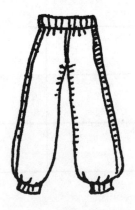

Getting Ready For School

Getting Dressed

After you choose your clothes, fold them neatly in your room, or lay them out on the floor in the form of a person. Have your mom or dad check the clothes you picked to make sure they match.

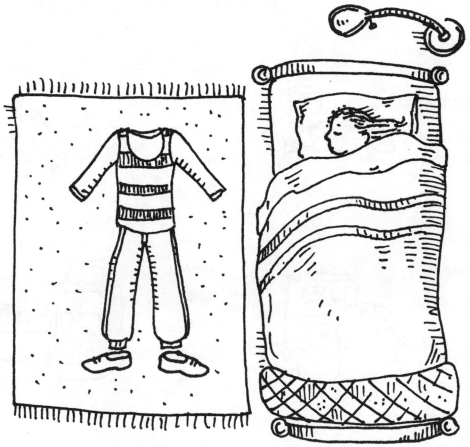

Making Breakfast

Breakfast is the most important meal of the day. A good breakfast will give you energy. It will help you do better in school. A good breakfast should have something from each of the four food groups.

Protein

eggs

peanut butter

cheese

lunch meat

Fruit

bananas

apples

oranges

raisins

berries

Grains

toast

cereal

crackers

Dairy

milk

cheese

yogurt

Make Breakfast Fun Without Cooking

Banana Boat–

This breakfast has something from each food group.

Protein: Peanut butter
Grains: Wheat bread
Dairy: Milk
Fruit: Banana

Make your own breakfast. Use something from each food group.

Protein: _____   **Dairy:** _____

Grains: _____   **Fruit:** _____

Foods to Choose

Here is a list of healthy foods you can use to make a lunch.

Protein

lunch meats

peanut butter

tuna

egg salad

cheese

nuts

Fruits & Vegetables

carrots

celery

cucumbers

tomatoes

apples

oranges

raisins

Dairy

milk

cheese

yogurt

butter

Grains

whole wheat bread

crackers

oatmeal cookies

corn chips

What's Missing

Here are some lunches a fourth grade student made. Add something to each lunch that will make it complete. Be sure every lunch has at least one item from each food group.

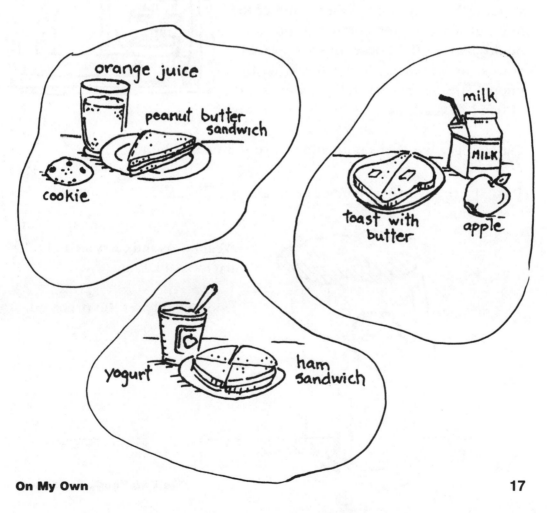

What to Wear

It is important to pick the right coat or jacket to wear to school. Have your parents hang a thermometer outside the kitchen window. You can use the thermometer to find out what the temperature is outside before leaving the house. In some places, you can find out what the weather is like by phone. The message will tell you what kind of day to expect.

Can you get weather information in your area by phone?_____

If so, list the weather number here. _____

Wear boots and carry an umbrella if it looks like rain.

Don't be all wet. Be prepared.

What's the Temperature?

70° or higher
You don't need a coat

55° to 70°
Wear a light jacket

35° to 55°
Wear a heavy coat

Under 35°
Wear a heavy coat, gloves, hat, and scarf

Don't Forget!

Planning ahead can make your mornings less rushed. Make a list of what you need to bring to school each day.

_____

_____

_____

_____

_____

_____

Now that you know what you need for school, put all your things together in one place before you go to bed. In the morning you will be ready and set to go.

Before You Leave

Here is a list of all the things you should do before you leave for school. Talk to your parents and add to this list if necessary.

1. Make sure the stove and oven are turned off.

2. Put all food away.

3. Put pets where they belong.

4. Make sure all windows are closed and locked.

5. _____

_____

6. _____

_____

Before leaving for school, check to make sure you have everything you need.

Chapter 2

After School

If you have to take care of yourself after school, there are a lot of things you need to know. The first thing you need to know is how to get home from school safely. Your parents have probably trusted you with a key. You need to know how to take care of your key and what to do if you lose it. Finally, once you get home, you need to be able to tell if your house is safe to enter. This chapter will teach you all these things.

Getting Home

Some children walk home from school. Other children ride in a car. Many children ride on a school bus or a city bus.

How do you get home from school?

_____ Walk

_____ Car

_____ School bus

_____ Public transportation

Have you ever gotten lost or missed your ride? _____

If you have, what did you do? _____

_____

What would you do if you did? _____

_____

24   **After School**

A Change of Plans?

Your parents expect you to come home from school a certain way. Do not change your plans without asking your parents.

You walk out the front door of your school and a friend of your father's drives up and asks you if you want a ride home. What should you say?

_____

_____

A friend asks you to walk home with him. He lives four blocks out of your way. It would take you about fifteen minutes longer to get home. What should you say?

_____

_____

A Map Home

Draw a map that shows how you get from school to your home. Label all the streets.

Draw a dotted line to show another way that you could get home if your regular route was blocked.

Emergency Card

Cut out the emergency card and fill in the information. Fold it on the dotted lines. Keep it with you when you leave the house. If you get lost or have an accident you may need this information.

School

School _____

Address _____

Phone _____

Teacher _____

Home

Address _____

_____

Phone _____

Work

Parents' names _____

_____

Work places _____

Phones _____

Friend

Name _____

Address _____

_____

Phone _____

Key Safety

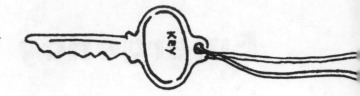

If you must come home to an empty house after school, you probably have a key that you use to let yourself inside. Some children keep their key at a neighbor's and pick it up on the way home from school so they know it's safe. But most children keep their key with them at all times.

If you keep your key with you, make sure it is secure so you don't lose it.

Wear it on a string or chain around your neck. If you wear your key around your neck, make sure you wear it inside your shirt so that no one can see it.

Pin it to the inside of your pocket.

Hook it on a key chain attached to your belt.

Where do you keep your key? _____

_____

Key Rules

Read the following rules for keeping your key safe. Write the reason for each rule.

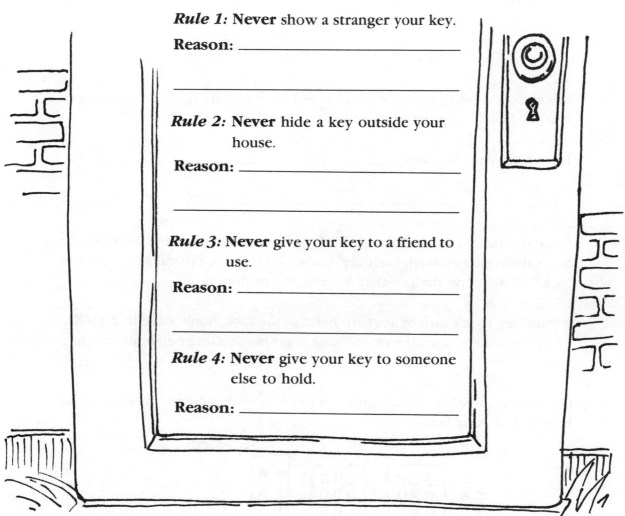

Rule 1: **Never** show a stranger your key.

Reason: _____

_____

Rule 2: **Never** hide a key outside your house.

Reason: _____

_____

Rule 3: **Never** give your key to a friend to use.

Reason: _____

_____

Rule 4: **Never** give your key to someone else to hold.

Reason: _____

Using Your Key

Trace your key.

Some keys look the same on both sides. Other keys are different. Some keys work right side up or upside down. Other keys only work one way.

How does your key work? _____

_____

Some doors have more than one lock and more than one key. If you need more than one key, mark each key. Put a "T" on the key that fits into the top lock and a "B" on the key that fits into the bottom lock.

If your key won't turn or starts to bend in the lock, don't force it. It might break and then you really won't be able to get inside. Get a neighbor to help you.

Before you come home to an empty house, make sure your parents teach you how to use your key.

30

Lost Key

No matter how careful you are, there is always a chance, that you might lose your key. You and your parents might decide to keep a spare key at a neighbor's just in case. If you do not have a spare key, *don't panic*. Go to a neighbor or a store and call one of your parents. Explain that you lost your key, and where you are. Follow your parent's directions.

Have you ever lost your key? _____

What happened? _____

_____

What would you do if you lost your key tomorrow? _____

_____

Safe to Enter?

Before you enter your house, look for any one of these things. They all mean your house is *not* safe to enter.

a ladder next to an upstairs window

an open window

a broken window

an open door

Would You Enter?

Look at the pictures of these houses. Decide if they are safe to enter.

___yes ___no

___yes ___no

___yes ___no

___yes ___no

Unsafe!
Now What?

If your house is unsafe to enter, go to a neighbor's or a friend's and have an adult check your house. If there are no adults around, do not go back to your house with your friends. Instead, call your parents or the police for advice.

Name and address of neighbor: _____

_____

Parents' work phone numbers: _____

Police phone number: _____

Safe!
Now What!

Once inside be sure to lock the door. Then go to the phone and check in with one of your parents or a neighbor to say you are safe at home.

What person do you check in with when you get home from school?

_____

Phone number: _____

Chapter 3

Using The Telephone

The telephone is your most important tool when you are home alone. It can put you in touch with your parents, neighbors, doctor, police, or fire department. It can help you feel less alone by letting you talk to your friends. The telephone can save your life in an emergency. This chapter will teach you how to use the telephone correctly.

Hello

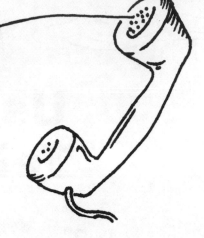

When answering the telephone, just say hello. **Never** tell anyone you are home alone. Instead say, "My mother is busy. May I take a message and have her call you back later?"

Read the following questions callers may ask you. What would you say if someone called and said:

Hi. Let me speak to your mother._____

_____

Are you home alone? _____

_____

Hi. This is Mrs. Jones. I need to talk to your mother about something important. Do you have her telephone number at work?_____

_____

Hi. Is your father home?_____

_____

Important Phone Numbers

Cut out this page. Post this list of important telephone numbers next to your telephone. Even if you know them all, it's important to post them. In an emergency, you might get excited and forget the very one you need.

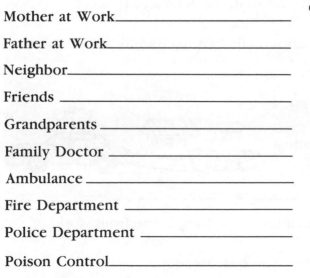

Mother at Work _____

Father at Work _____

Neighbor _____

Friends _____

Grandparents _____

Family Doctor _____

Ambulance _____

Fire Department _____

Police Department _____

Poison Control _____

Operator _____

When Should You Call the Police Department?

Here is a list of things that might happen when you are home alone.

Under which of these circumstances should you call the police?

_____1. The toilet overflows.

_____2. There is a knock at the door.

_____3. You answer the phone and someone tells a dirty joke.

_____4. You come home from school to find a broken window and the front door open.

_____5. The electricity goes out.

_____6. A fire starts in the kitchen.

_____7. Your dog runs away.

_____8. Your mother is ten minutes late getting home from work.

_____9. You're scared. You think you hear someone outside.

_____10. A stranger follows you home from school.   (4,10)

What Should You Say?

Fill in the blanks so that when you call the police department you will know what to say.

First, tell them what the problem is:

_____

_____

Then say "My name is": _____

"I live at": _____

And if you live in an apartment, say "I live in apartment number": _____

Do not hang up. Wait for further directions from the police. They might want to tell you what to do, or ask for more information.

Calling the Fire Department

If there is a fire at your house, leave your house immediately Call the fire department from a friend's house or a public telephone.

Say: "I want to report a fire at": _____

_____

(Be sure to give both your street address and the town in which you live.)

Then the dispatcher will say:

"What's your name?": _____

"What's the phone number from which you are calling?":_____

"What's burning?":_____

He or she might also ask, "What are the closest main streets to the fire?":

_____

Be sure to remain calm and speak clearly so the dispatcher can write the information correctly.

The Operator

The operator is the easiest person to reach in case of an emergency. All you need to do is dial 0. If you can not find the number you need in an emergency, just call the operator. Here are pictures of two different phones. Number the dials. Color the button or hole you would use to reach the operator.

Operator Services

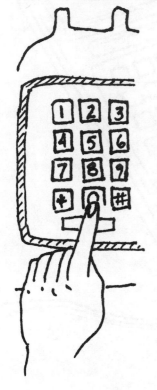

Here is a list of some of the things the operator can do.

✔ Dial a number for you.

✔ Check to see if the number you are calling is really busy.

✔ Connect you with the police department or fire department.

✔ Call an ambulance or the poison control center for you.

✔ Tell you the area code of another city.

✔ Tell you the time.

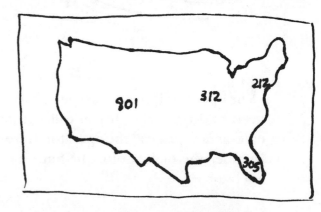

Directory Assistance

If you want to find out the telephone number of someone who lives nearby, don't call the operator, dial 411. When the directory assistance operator answers, be sure to have a pencil and paper ready to write down the number. To find out someone's telephone number you have tell the operator the person's first and last name, and the city in which that person lives.

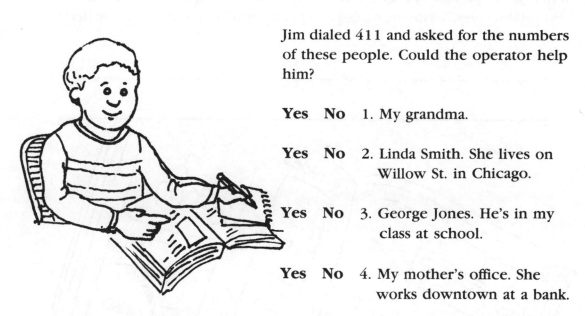

Jim dialed 411 and asked for the numbers of these people. Could the operator help him?

Yes **No** 1. My grandma.

Yes **No** 2. Linda Smith. She lives on Willow St. in Chicago.

Yes **No** 3. George Jones. He's in my class at school.

Yes **No** 4. My mother's office. She works downtown at a bank.

Before you call directory assistance, try to find the number in the phone book. In some areas directory assistance is not free. Your parents have to pay every time you ask for help.

What's the Number?

When you get a telephone, you get two phone books. One has yellow pages and is called the Yellow Pages. The other one has White Pages and is called the White Pages. The businesses in your area are listed in the Yellow Pages. They are grouped by the kind of things they sell or fix. Find the Yellow Pages at your house. Look up **Bicycles-Retail**. You will find it under the letter "B" in the Yellow Pages. You will see a list of all the stores in your area that sell bicycles. Write the names and phone numbers of two of them here.

_____   _____

_____   _____

The White Pages

The White Pages gives a list of businesses and people. The White Pages lists names in alphabetical order. To look up someone's name in the White Pages you first look for their last name. Try to find your family's phone number in the White Pages. Look under your last name and then for the first name of your father or mother.

Did you find it?_____

Now try to find the number of three of your friends. Be sure to look under their last name and then their parent's first name.

Friend's Name	Father's Name	Phone Number
_____	_____	_____
_____	_____	_____
_____	_____	_____

A Broken Telephone

If you pick up the phone and there is no
dial tone, check other phones in the house.
Make sure they are all hung up correctly.
Wait five minutes and try the phone again.
Sometimes the reason there is no dial tone
is that many people are trying to use their
phones at the same time.

How many phones do you have in your house?_____

Where are they located? _____

_____

Really Broken?
Now What?

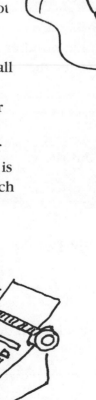

Once you decide your phone is really broken, there are two things you can do. Discuss them with your parents and circle either plan A or plan B.

A. Stay calm, wait until an adult comes home, and explain that the phone is not working. Do not go outside.

B. Go to a friend's or neighbor's house. Call the operator and explain that the telephone is not working. The operator will ask for your telephone number, so make sure you know it. Then, call your mom or dad at work and say the phone is not working. They may be trying to reach you.

Crazy Calls

Sometimes you will get a call that you do not understand from someone. It might be a wrong number. Maybe it is some kids like you who are home alone having fun. If the person on the other end of the phone says something that frightens you, hang up and call the operator right away. Be sure to tell your parents, too. If you get many crazy calls, your parents might want to have your telephone number changed. *Never* tell a crazy caller that you are home alone.

Have you ever gotten a crazy call?_____

What did the caller say?_____

_____

What did you do? _____

_____

What would you do now? _____

_____

On My Own

Sometimes you will be home alone, and your mom or dad can't be reached by telephone. Maybe they are on their way home or at a store. When this is the case, you are really on your own. That is why you need the name and number of two adults to call in case of emergency. These are your parent back-ups. They can be friends or relatives. Think about who you would like to have as your parent back-ups. Write their names and phone numbers here.

Name_____

Phone Number _____

Name_____

Phone Number _____

Chapter 4

Snacks

Many children make snacks when they come home from school. Others make snacks when they are alone during the evening. This chapter will teach you a few tricks for making nutritious and delicious snacks. It will also teach you how to work in the kitchen.

My Favorites

Make a list of your favorite snacks.

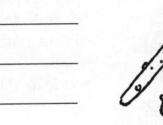

Good Snacks

To find out how many of your favorite snacks are good snacks do this:

1. Cross out all "My Favorites" that you would have to cook.
       (hamburgers & hotdogs)

2. Cross out all "My Favorites" that have a lot of sugar.
       (cookies, cakes, & candies)

3. Cross out all "My Favorites" that are fried.
       (potato chips & corn chips)

How many snacks are left on your list?_____

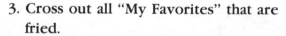

Who Is Ready to Fix a Snack?

Look at the pictures and circle the children who are following the Ready To Fix a Snack rules.

Rule 1: Wear old clothes. ***Don't*** get your school clothes dirty.

Rule 2: Wash your face and hands. ***Don't*** get dirt in the food.

Rule 3: Make sure you have everything you need before you begin. ***Don't*** start to fix a snack and find out something is missing.

Safety in the Kitchen

Circle the pictures of the children who are following the safety rules.

Rule 1: Eat no snacks you have to bake. *Don't* use the stove when you are home alone.

Rule 2: Use a butter knife. *Don't* use sharp knives when you are alone.

Rule 3: Electrical appliances are dangerous. *Don't* use them when fixing a snack alone.

Rule 4: Clean up spills right away. *Don't* slip and fall on something that was spilled.

Ready Snacks

Some foods are good quick snacks. You don't have to cut or cook them. They are ready to eat. Draw a picture of each of these snack foods.

Carrots	Bananas
Celery	Berries
Apples	Raisins
Oranges	Nuts
Pears	Yogurt
Grapes	Pretzels

Yucky Snacks

Cross out the snacks that are not good for you.

Easy, No-Cook Snacks

Here are the recipes for three snacks that are easy to make and fun to eat. You do not have to use the stove to make them. Try one.

Honey Nut Spread   Mix one tablespoon of honey with one tablespoon of peanut butter. Spread on bread.

Snowy Log   Use a butter knife to fill a piece of celery with cream cheese. Top with raisins.

Fruit Salad   Cut up one orange, one apple, and one banana into a small bowl. Mix one teaspoon of sugar or honey and three teaspoons of water together in a cup. Pour over cut up fruit.

Old Stand-Bys

Here are some pairs of foods that go well together.
Add a few of your own pairs to the list.

Peanut Butter and Jelly

Cheese and Crackers

Graham Crackers and Milk

Apples and Cheese

_____

_____

_____

Peanut Butter on Parade....

Here are some good things you can make using peanut butter and other snack foods.

Peanut Butter Faces　Spread peanut butter on a round cracker. Use raisins to make a face.

Peanut Butter Apple　Use a butter knife to cut an apple in four pieces. Cut out the core. Spread peanut butter on each of the four pieces. Stick them back together. Put in the refrigerator to chill.

Peanut Butter Designs　Spread peanut butter on a slice of bread. Decorate with sunflower seeds, and raisins.

And Parade

Peanut Butter Submarine   Peel a banana. Slice it down the center with a butter knife. Stuff it with peanut butter. Decorate with raisins and nuts.

Peanut Butter Spears   Clean a piece of celery. Stuff it with peanut butter. Decorate the stuffed celery with raisins.

Peanut Butter Pizza   Toast a slice of bread. Spread with peanut butter. Sprinkle with chopped fruit. Use oranges, peaches, bananas, apples or pineapple.

Puzzle Apple

Use a butter knife to change an apple into a magic puzzle.

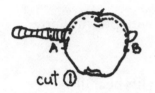

cut ①

Make a slit halfway down the center of your apple from the top.

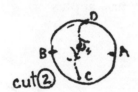

cut ②

Turn it upside down and cut half way in so the two slits form a cross.

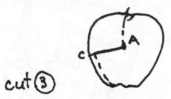

cut ③

Make a cut that connects point A with point C.

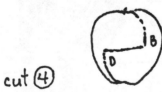

cut ④

Then connect point B with point D. Be sure to make cuts deep enough so apple can pull apart easily.

Now you are ready to enjoy your puzzle apple.

Cleaning Up

When you finish cooking, be sure to clean up. When your parents come home from work, they do not want to see a messy kitchen. After you finish cooking, check to make sure you did everything on this list.

_____1. Washed the dishes.

_____2. Washed the counter.

_____3. Put the dishes away.

_____4. Wrapped or covered leftover food.

_____5. Put leftovers in the refrigerator.

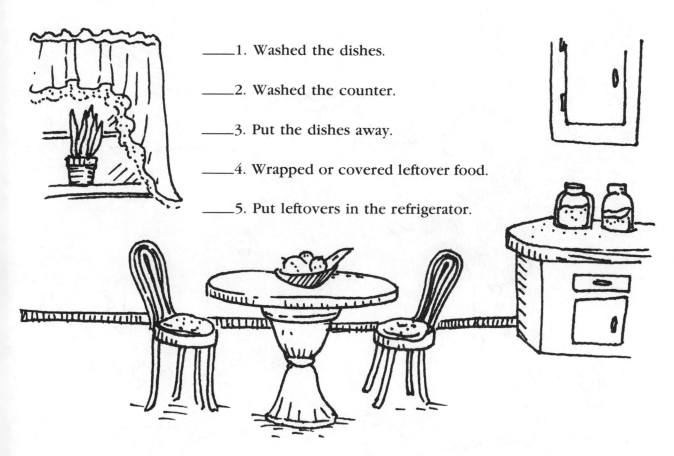

Chapter 5

Outside
Play

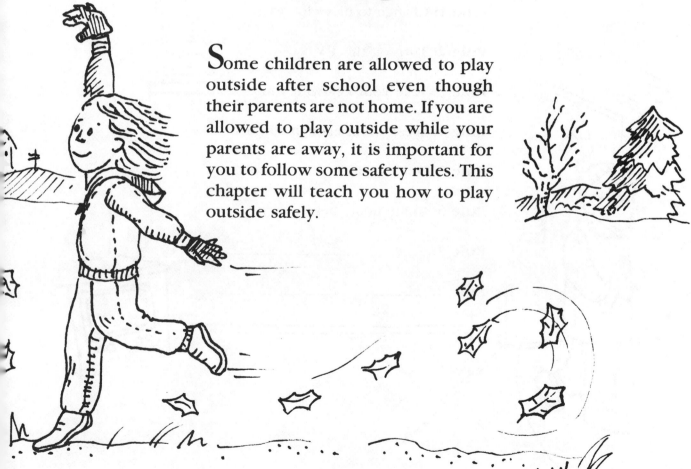

Some children are allowed to play outside after school even though their parents are not home. If you are allowed to play outside while your parents are away, it is important for you to follow some safety rules. This chapter will teach you how to play outside safely.

Rules

When you play outside, follow these rules. Discuss them with your parents. Add any rules they have to the list.

Rule 1: Change to play clothes.

Rule 2: Turn off the T.V.

Rule 3: Take your key with you.

Rule 4: Wear warm enough clothes.

Rule 5: Don't go in anyone's house.

Rule 6: Come home before dark.

Rule 7: _____

Rule 8: _____

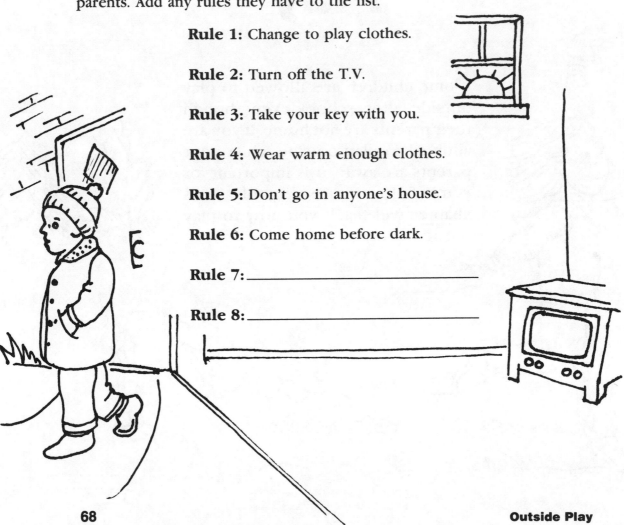

Where to Play

Draw a map of your neighborhood. Draw a circle around the places where you are allowed to play. Cross out the places where you are not allowed to play.

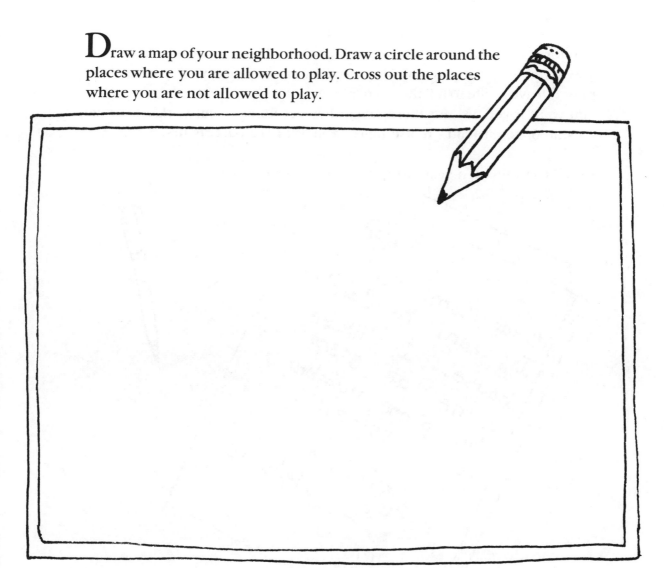

Telling Your Parents

Before you go outside, call your parents to ask them if you can go outside. If you are allowed to play outside and you can not reach your parents by phone, leave a note to tell them where you went. A note will tell them where you went if you are not there when they get home from work. **Never** go outside or to a friend's house unless you ask your parents first.

Here is a note a ten-year-old girl wrote to her mother.

Writing A Note

Write a practice note to your parents. On your note write the time the note was written, where you went, whom you are with, and the time you will get home. Put the note where your parents will see it.

Super Bike

Bikes are fun, but they can be dangerous. A bike that is in good condition and has good safety equipment is safe to ride.

Check your bike to make sure it is safe to ride. Circle **Yes** or **No** for each question on the list. If you answer every question **Yes**, then your bike is in super condition.

Yes   No   1. The seat on my bike is tight. It does not wiggle.

Yes   No   2. The handlebars on my bike are tight. They do not wiggle.

Yes   No   3. My bike has a headlight that works.

Yes   No   4. My bike has a horn that works.

Yes   No   5. The pedals on my bike are not broken.

Yes   No   6. My bike has a chain guard.

Yes   No   7. The brakes stop my bike quickly.

Yes   No   8. There are reflectors on my bike.

Yes   No   9. The tires on my bike are in good condition.

Yes   No   10. All the spokes are on the wheels.

Ace Driving

$\mathbf{I}$t is easy to learn how to ride a bike. But it takes a lot of practice to be an ace driver. Here are five driving skills for you to practice. An ace driver can do them all.

Take a piece of chalk and draw the following lines on the side walk, your driveway, or in an empty parking lot. Practice these driving skills until you can do them perfectly. Try to do them without skidding or putting your feet on the ground.

1. Draw a straight line. Ride on the line slowly.

2. Draw an **X** on the sidewalk. Stop at the **X**.

3. Draw a large figure **8**. Make it as wide as two cars. Ride on the line.

4. Draw a zigzag on the sidewalk. Ride on the line.

5. Draw an oval. Ride on the oval.

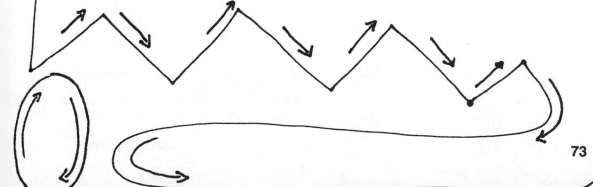

Dogs and...

Having a dog bark at you or chase you is scary. If a dog runs toward you while you are walking home or playing outside, **Do Not Run**. Keep walking. Running will only make a dog chase you more.

Never chase or pet a strange dog. Many dogs are not used to children. When you chase them or try to pet them they may become frightened. A dog that is frightened may try to bite you.

If a dog bothers you when you are playing outside or walking home from school, remember where the dog lives. When your parents get home, ask them to talk to the dog's owner. Most towns and cities have laws that say dogs are not allowed to run loose.

How many dogs live in your neighborhood?_____

Write their names and what kinds of dogs they are here:

Name   **Kind**

_____   _____

_____   _____

_____   _____

_____   _____

Other Animals

When playing outside, the best rule to follow is do not pet or feed strange animals. The lizard or squirrel that plays in your yard may look friendly, but it is a wild animal. A bite from even a small animal can be very dangerous.

Make a list of the kinds of animals that live in your neighborhood.

Strangers

If you play outside, do not talk to strangers. Do not get in a car with a stranger. Do not tell strangers you are home alone or show them your keys.

If you think you are being followed, go in a store or to a friend's house. Do not go to your house. If you live in an apartment, do not get in an elevator with someone who makes you feel uncomfortable. Wait for the next elevator.

What would you do in the following situations?

Someone is following you home from school?_____

_____

Someone in a car asks you to get in. That person offers you candy.

_____

_____

Auto Safety

When you play outside, follow these rules.

Rule 1: Cross the street at the corner.

Rule 2: Obey traffic signs and signals.

Rule 3: Walk facing traffic.

Rule 4: Wear light colored clothing when walking at night.

These children are not following the rules. What are they doing wrong?

1. _____

2. _____

3. _____

Thunderstorms

If you are outside and a thunderstorm starts, go inside. If you are near your house, go there. If not, go to a friend's house or a large building like a store or school. If you are stuck outside, stay away from metal objects, trees, hilltops, or a lake. Here is a picture of a child stuck in a storm. Where should he go?

Outside Play

Water Safety

If you are lucky, you have a pool, or live near the ocean or a lake. Swimming and boating are fun. But you should only go swimming or boating when an adult is present. Name three things that could happen if you went swimming or boating alone.

1. _____

2. _____

3. _____

Chapter 6

Inside Activities

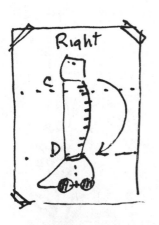

How do you spend your time when you are alone? Do you watch television? Or do you look out the window waiting for your parents to come home? There are many things you can do when you are alone that are fun and useful. This chapter will help you plan the time you spend alone. It will give you ideas of things you can do when you are home alone.

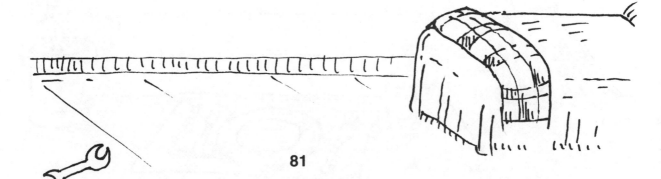

Chores

Chores are not all bad. A few chores will keep you busy. Chores help make the time you spend alone seem shorter. Doing a few chores can help your parents. When they come home from work, they will have more time to spend with you. Here is a list of chores that are safe and easy. Add a few of your own ideas to the list. Check two that you would like to do. Talk about them with your parents.

_____1. Make the beds.

_____2. Wash the breakfast dishes.

_____3. Dust the furniture.

_____4. Sweep the kitchen floor.

_____5. Clean your room.

_____6. Set the table.

_____7. _____

_____8. _____

Homework

Teachers give you homework so that you can practice what you learned in school. Homework is something you can do by yourself. You don't need your parents' help. Do your homework when you are alone and let your parents check it when they come home from work.

Here is a homework chart. When you finish your homework, draw a star in the right box. If you have no homework, draw a smiley face. If you do not finish your homework, draw a sad face. This chart can help you keep track of your homework for two weeks. If you get all stars and smiles you are a *Homework Star!*

	Monday	*Tuesday*	*Wednesday*	*Thursday*	*Friday*
Week 1					
Week 2					

Rules for Free-Time Activities

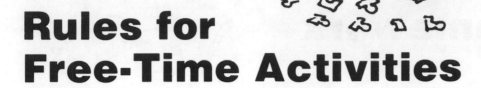

Here are some rules for free-time activities. After each rule, write the reason for the rule. The first one is done for you.

Rule 1. Do *not* use sharp objects or electrical appliances.

Reason: You might hurt yourself.

Rule 2. Make sure you have enough time to finish the activity.

Reason: _____

_____

Rule 3. Do *not* make a lot of noise.

Reason: _____

_____

Rule 4. Clean up when you are done.

Reason: _____

_____

Hobbies

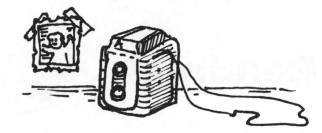

Make a list of things you enjoy doing by yourself. Put a star by the activities that are safe to do when your parents are not home. Include some of these activities when you plan your weekly schedule.

1. _____

2. _____

3. _____

4. _____

5. _____

Reading

Reading is a great free-time activity. Plan a weekly visit to the library. Get out new books and take back the ones you have read. Ask your parents to take you on Saturday morning or one evening when they get home from work. Go the same day each week.

Keep a list of the books you finish. Read five books and become a **Super Reader.**

Name of Book	Author

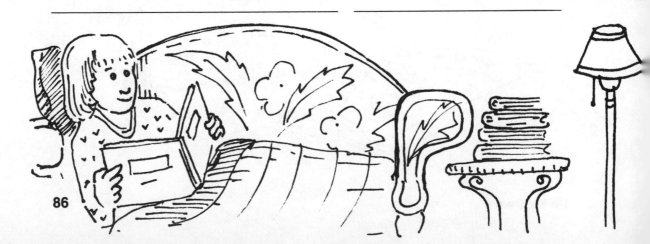

Letters

It is fun to send mail and to get mail back. Write a letter to your grandparents, cousins, or friends. Write a welcome home note to your parents or a thank-you note to the postman. If you enjoy writing letters or getting mail, sign up for a pen pal.

List people you could write to when you have free time.

_____   _____

_____   _____

_____   _____

P.S. If you want a pen pal, send a self-addressed stamped envelope for an application to:

Pen Pals   or   Student Letter Exchange
22 Batterymarch Street   910 4th Street
Boston, Mass. 02109   Austin, Texas 55912

Television

Television can be fun. It can teach you new things. Here are some rules for watching television. Write the reason for each rule.

Rule 1. Do not sit close to the television.

Reason: _____

_____

Rule 2. Do not watch too much television.

Reason: _____

_____

Rule 3. Do not watch scarey television programs.

Reason: _____

_____

Television Favorites

Most people have favorite television shows. What are some of yours?

Get a copy of the T.V. guide. Find out what shows are on Monday. Write down your three favorite shows. Now do the same thing for the rest of the week.

Monday   *Tuesday*   *Wednesday*

_____   _____   _____

_____   _____   _____

_____   _____   _____

        Thursday   *Friday*

        _____   _____

        _____   _____

        _____   _____

Arts and Crafts

There are many of things you can make with objects you find around the house. Try some of these ideas.

Cardboard Flute

Take a paper towel tube and punch three holes in it. Cover the end of the tube with wax paper and use a rubber band to hold the paper. Hum a tune into your new flute.

Masks

Cut two eyes out of a brown paper bag. Cut two half-circles for your shoulders. Color the bag to look like your favorite monster.

Potato Stamps

Use a butter knife to cut a potato in half. Cut a design in the potato, dip it in paint, and stamp it on paper. Use your potato stamp to turn brown paper bags into place mats or wrapping paper.

Other Free-Time Ideas

If you still can't think of anything you can do when you are home alone, try some of these ideas.

Fixing Food: Fixing food is a good way to pass the time. Make a salad for dinner or try some of the no cook recipes in the snacks chapter. Be sure not to use the stove and always clean up your mess.

Puzzles: Save your allowance and buy a jigsaw puzzle. Put the puzzle where you can leave it out for a few days and where it will not be in the way.

Diary: Keep a diary. Get an old notebook and write down what you do each day. Diaries are fun to write and to read.

Videogames: A computer or a videogame system will give you hours of fun. Use a notebook to keep track of your high scores.

Puzzle Books: There are all types of puzzles: crosswords, word searches, secret codes, and mazes. Get a book of puzzles and try some.

Pets: Pets can provide hours of fun. Why not brush your cat, or teach your dog a new trick?

Collections: You can collect anything. Collections are fun. You can trade, sort, or look at the objects in a collection. Some of the most popular children's collections are baseball cards, coins, stamps, and stickers.

Planning Your Day

You will get more done when you are alone if you plan your day ahead of time. Figure out how much time you are going to be alone. Then write down what you are going to do. Do the things you have to do, like your homework or chores, first. Do things like watching television or playing with your friends, after you finish doing what you have to do.

Here is a schedule Lisa made up.

2:45-3:00   Change clothes.
             Have a snack.

3:00-3:30   Chores.

3:30-4:30   Homework.

4:30-5:30   Watch television.

5:30   Mom comes home.

Inside Activities

Schedule

Plan the time you have to stay alone.

Time	Activity
_____	_____
_____	_____
_____	_____
_____	_____
_____	_____

Chapter 7

Scared?

When you are home alone, you might hear a noise that scares you. Or something might happen that scares you. This chapter will teach you some things you can do to make you feel safer when you stay alone.

Safety Inspection

In most places a policeman will come to your house and do a free safety inspection. The policeman will tell you how you can make your house safer. Ask your parents to call the nearest police station and ask the police to inspect your house or apartment. Write down the suggestions they make on this page. Cross them off when your parents do them.

Safe

Here are some things that will make your house or apartment more safe. Check them when your house has them.

_____ 1. ***Deadbolt locks.*** Have your parents put deadbolt locks on the door.

_____ 2. ***Safety chain.*** Have your parents put a chain lock on the door so that no one can come in the house when you are home alone.

_____ 3. ***Window locks.*** Have your parents put locks on all the windows on the first floor. They should also put locks on windows that are near a fire escape.

_____ 4. ***Low bushes.*** Have your parents cut the bushes in front of the house so no one can hide in them.

_____ 5. ***Outside lights.*** Have your parents put lights outside your house so when it gets dark early in the winter, it won't feel so dark.

Alarm Systems

An alarm system warns you in case of danger. If someone tries to break into your house, a burglar alarm will make a loud noise. Some burglar alarms ring at the police station. Other alarm systems ring only at your home. When they ring, you call the police. Burglar alarms are very expensive. But if you spend a lot of time home alone, or if your parents think your neighborhood is not safe, it might be a good idea to get one.

Fill in the blanks.

A burglar alarm warns you in case of

_____

A burglar alarm makes a loud

_____

When a burglar alarm goes off, call the

_____

Scared?

Dogs

Dogs are great alarm systems. They hear noises people can't hear. Dogs will bark and scare a burglar away. Children who are home alone and have dogs often feel safer than children who do not have dogs. They feel the dogs protect them and are good company.

If you have a dog, draw a picture of your dog. If you don't have a dog but would like one, draw a picture of the dog you would like to have.

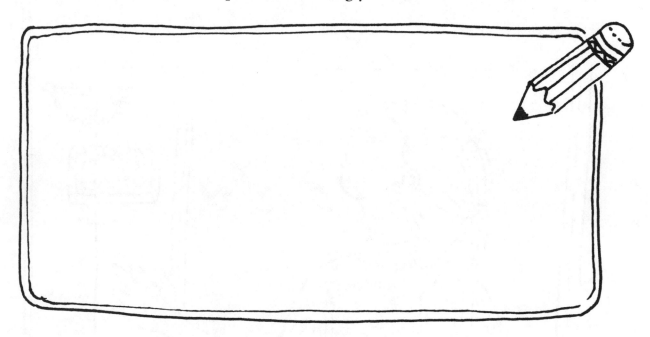

What kind of dog is it? _____

Peek Hole

A peek hole can let you see who is at the door without them seeing you. Have your parents put a peek hole down low so that you can see out easily. Then if there is a knock at the door, you will know who it is. Make a list with your parents of which people you are allowed to let in the house.

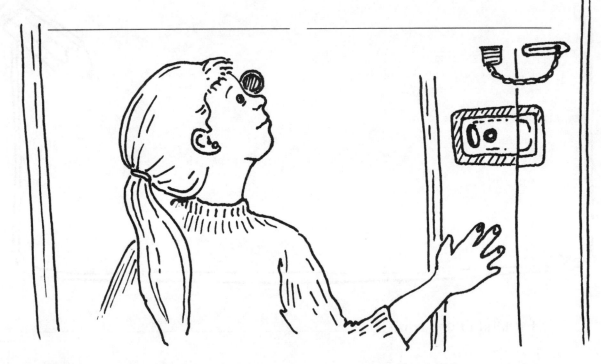

Scared?

Knock at the Door

If there is a knock at the door, you can follow either plan A or plan B. Decide with your parents which plan is best for you.

Plan A

Do not open the door for anyone. If there is knock at the door, sit quietly and pretend no one is home. If you have a peep hole, you can look out it. Stay away from the windows where you can be seen.

Plan B

If there is a knock at the door, ask, "Who is it?" Never open the door unless you know who it is. If the person is not on your OK list, say your mother is in the shower. If you are not sure what to do, call a parent or a neighbor.

People to Phone

If you are home alone, and you are feeling lonely or scared, the phone can be a great help. Talking to a friend on the phone can make the time go by quickly and help you forget you are afraid. Ask your friends for their phone numbers. Take this book to school and write them in it. The next time you are afraid or lonely, it will be easy to call one of them.

Friend's Name	*Phone Number*
_____	_____
_____	_____
_____	_____
_____	_____
_____	_____

Contact

You will feel safer if there is someone nearby you can go to if you get scared. A good contact person is an adult who lives nearby and is home when you are alone. A relative or a close friend are both good contact people. Decide with your parents who would be a good contact person. Once you decide on a contact person, you and your parents should go visit them. Tell that person that you are going to be home alone in the afternoon. Ask if you can come to his or her house when you feel scared.

Make a list of three people you'd like to have as your contact person. Discuss these with your parents.

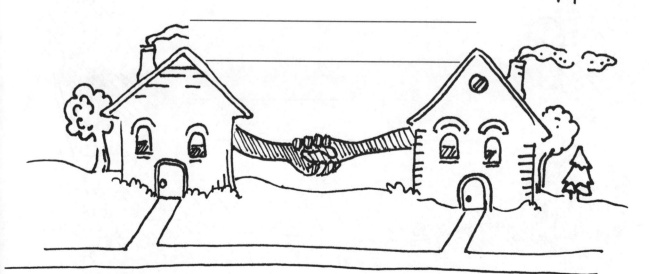

_____

_____

_____

Dark

In the winter the days are shorter and it gets dark earlier. If you are alone after school, you might be alone when it's dark. Are you afraid of the dark? Nothing changes just because it's dark. Everything is exactly the same as when it was light. You just can't see as well. It takes about ½ hour for your eyes to adjust to darkness. If you are afraid of the dark, ask your parents to put a light outside your house or apartment. Put curtains that you can close at night on the windows so that no one can see in your house.

Make a list of the things that frighten you. Talk about the things on this list with your parents.

Scared?

Noises...Noises... Noises...

When you are home alone, you might hear a noise that frightens you. Most children are frightened by noises that they can't explain. If you live in the country, the noise you hear outside might be a tree branch tapping your window or a raccoon tipping over your garbage can. If you live in a city, there are lots of sounds: people outside talking, cars driving by, or people walking upstairs.

Most noises can be explained. If you hear a noise that scares you, remember it. Describe it to your parents when they get home. Ask them to explain it to you. When your parents are home, listen for the noise that scared you. Point it out to them so they can explain it to you.

Turn off the T.V., radio and record player. Sit quietly in a comfortable chair. Close your eyes for five minutes. Listen to all the sounds you hear.

Break-ins

If you hear someone trying to break in your house either at a door or window, it is time to act quickly. You might hear a window break, or someone trying to force a door or window open. If you do, get out of the house another way. Go to a neighbor's and call the police.

You hear someone break your living room window. How

would you get out of your house? _____

_____

You hear someone breaking in the front door. How would

you get out of your house? _____

_____

Scared?

Trapped?

If you can't get out safely, call the police. Talk calmly. Tell the police your first and last name, your address and phone number. Tell them that you need help right away since there is a **burglary in progress**. Lock yourself in a room and wait **quietly** for the police. Do not walk around.

If none of the rooms of your house locks, ask your parents to put a lock on one of the doors. It's also a good idea to have a telephone in the room that locks so that you can call the police from there.

Where would you hide if you were trapped in the house during a robbery?

_____

Is there a phone in that room? _____

Do you remember the phone number of the police? _____

Chapter 8

Fire Safety

Every year over twelve thousand people die in fires in the United States. Many of these fires are started by children. Some happen when children are home alone. This chapter will help you prevent fires. It will teach you what to do if a fire starts while you are home alone.

Safety Check

The best way to protect yourself against a fire in your home is to have a safety check. Answer the following questions to get a safety rating on your house. Answer each question **Yes** or **No**.

Yes **No**   1. Is paint stored in tightly closed containers?

Yes **No**   2. Do extension cords run under the rugs?

Yes **No**   3. Do you have a fire extinguisher?

Yes **No**   4. Does your family allow smoking in bed?

Yes **No**   5. Is gasoline stored in safety approved cans?

Yes **No**   6. Do you put coins behind old fuses?

Yes **No**   7. Do you have a smoke detector?

Yes **No**   8. Do you overload electrical outlets?

The answers to questions 2, 4, 6, & 8 should be no.
The answers to questions 1, 3, 5, & 7 should be yes.

A score of 7 or 8 correct answers is excellent.

Fire Safety

Matches

Many children play with matches after school. Playing with matches can cause fires, injuries and even death. A dropped match can start a household fire. In order to make sure this doesn't happen to you, don't play with matches. If the lights go out, use a flashlight. Matches and candles are both too dangerous.

Make a list of five things that could happen if you played with matches.

1. _____

2. _____

3. _____

4. _____

5. _____

Smoke Detector

Most deaths by fire happen at night when everyone is sleeping. A smoke detector will wake you when there is a fire. It will give you time to get out of the house safely. You should have a smoke detector on every floor of your house. The best place to put smoke detectors is between the bedrooms and the rest of the house.

Do you have a smoke detector in your house?_____

Where is it? _____

Fire Safety

Fire Extinguishers

Every house should have a small fire extinguisher. Not every fire extinguisher can put out every type of fire. There are different types of fire extinguishers. The people who make fire extinguishers mark them. This way you know what type they are and what kind of fires they will put out.

Do you have a fire extinguisher at your house?_____

Where is it kept? _____

Read the label and find out:

What type of fire extinguisher is it?_____

What type of fires will it put out? _____

_____

Never use the fire extinguisher to put out a fire. It is too dangerous.

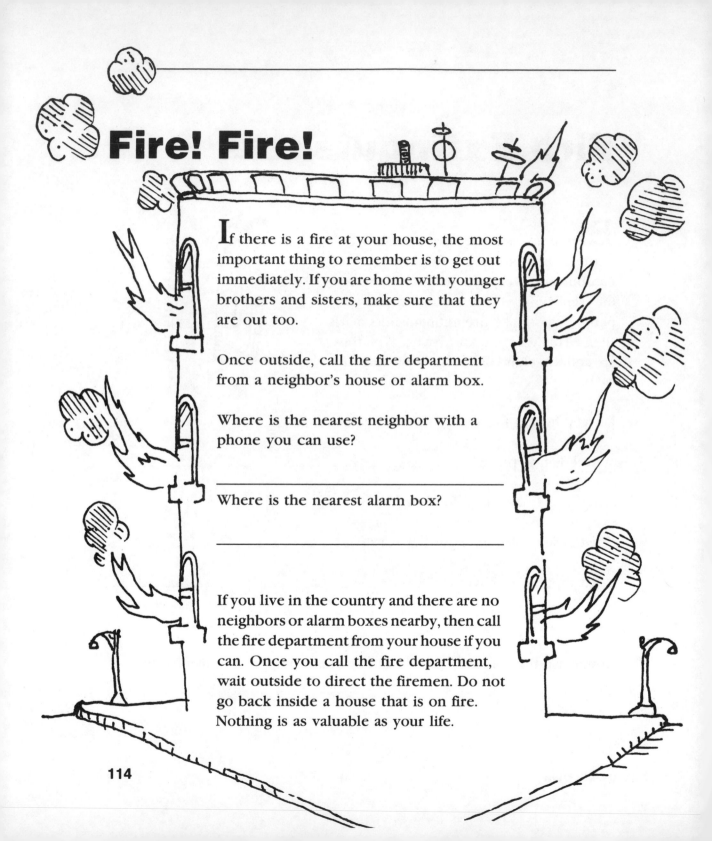

Fire! Fire!

If there is a fire at your house, the most important thing to remember is to get out immediately. If you are home with younger brothers and sisters, make sure that they are out too.

Once outside, call the fire department from a neighbor's house or alarm box.

Where is the nearest neighbor with a phone you can use?

_____

Where is the nearest alarm box?

_____

If you live in the country and there are no neighbors or alarm boxes nearby, then call the fire department from your house if you can. Once you call the fire department, wait outside to direct the firemen. Do not go back inside a house that is on fire. Nothing is as valuable as your life.

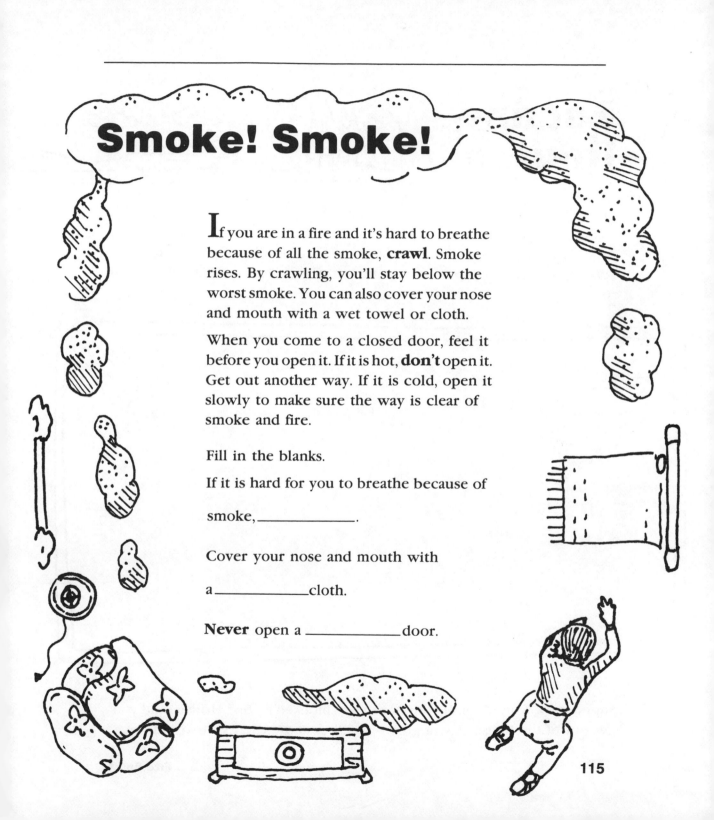

Smoke! Smoke!

If you are in a fire and it's hard to breathe because of all the smoke, **crawl**. Smoke rises. By crawling, you'll stay below the worst smoke. You can also cover your nose and mouth with a wet towel or cloth.

When you come to a closed door, feel it before you open it. If it is hot, **don't** open it. Get out another way. If it is cold, open it slowly to make sure the way is clear of smoke and fire.

Fill in the blanks.

If it is hard for you to breathe because of

smoke, _____.

Cover your nose and mouth with

a _____ cloth.

Never open a _____ door.

Escape Routes

Getting out of a house or apartment during a fire is not always easy. To make sure you have an escape plan, draw a floor plan of your house or apartment. Use a red crayon or pencil to draw an escape plan from each room.

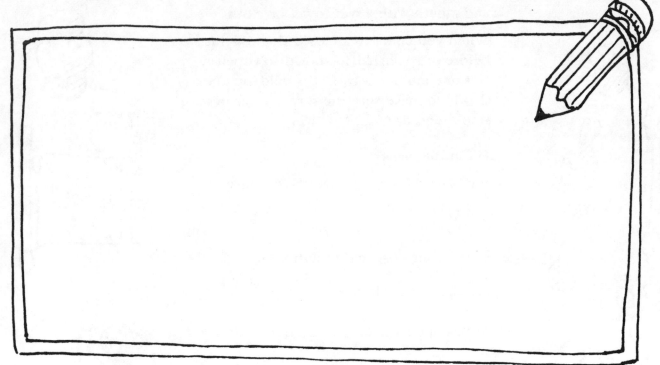

Suppose the front door of your house was blocked by fire. How would you get out of the house? Use a green pencil to show what you would do.

Upstairs

Suppose you live on the fifth floor of an apartment building or you are trapped on the second floor of your house, when a fire starts. How will you get out?

Check your house to see if you have at least one of the following.

_____1. A window with a fire escape outside it.

_____2. A window that has a porch roof just below it.

_____3. A window with a rope ladder attached to it.

Remember, if you live in an apartment, **never** use an elevator if there is a fire.

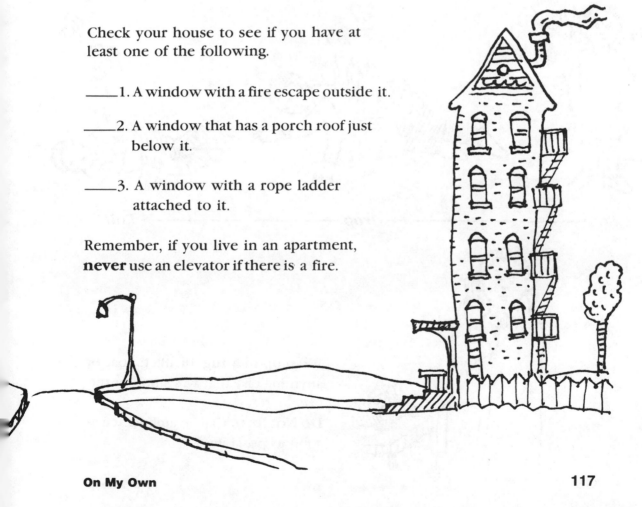

Clothing Fires

If your clothing catches on fire when you are home alone,

Stop ─────────────────────▶ *Drop* ─────────────────▶ *Roll*

Wrap up in a rug, blanket, coat or anything else that will smother the fire.

Do Not Run. Call an ambulance as soon as possible.

Cooking Fires

Most parents tell their children not to cook when they are home alone because they are afraid of fire. If your parents do let you cook, be careful.

If a fire starts in a pan on the stove, place the lid on the pot. The fire should go out in a couple of minutes. When you start cooking, place the lid near the pot. This way, if there is a fire, you will be ready.

Here is a picture of some pots on a stove.
Draw their lids next to them so they will be ready in case of a fire.

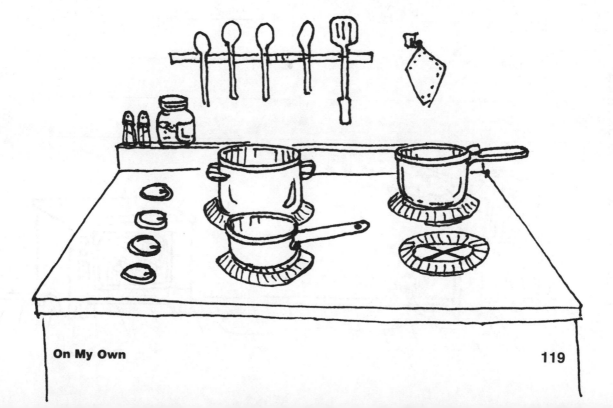

Electrical Fires

If an electrical appliance or the television starts to smoke, pull out the plug. If you can not pull out the plug **safely**, call the fire department. If an appliance or wiring catches on fire, call the fire department immediately. Do **not** try to put out an electrical fire with water.

Look around your house. Make a list of all the things that are plugged into an electrical socket all the time. Any of these things could start an electrical fire.

Fire Safety

Safe

The important thing to remember is that you are more important that your house or anything in it. In case of a fire, don't hurt yourself trying to put it out. Get out right away and call the fire department. Once outside, don't go back inside to get anything.

Chapter 9

First Aid

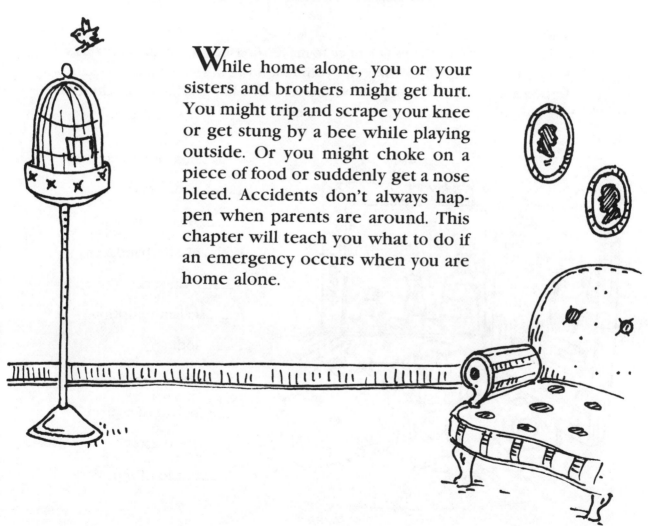

While home alone, you or your sisters and brothers might get hurt. You might trip and scrape your knee or get stung by a bee while playing outside. Or you might choke on a piece of food or suddenly get a nose bleed. Accidents don't always happen when parents are around. This chapter will teach you what to do if an emergency occurs when you are home alone.

First Aid Kit

Here is a list of the things you need to make a first aid kit. Check them off as you get them. Place all the things for your first aid kit in a shoe box. Decorate the box and place it in a safe place. If you get hurt while you are home alone, you will know where to get what you need.

_____box of bandages

_____gauze pads

_____small scissors

_____elastic bandages

_____tweezers

_____calamine lotion

_____iodine

_____thermometer

_____bottle of aspirin

_____ice pack

_____bottle of ipecac

First Aid

Safety Supplies

What are these safety supplies for? Match each to what it is used for.

Bandages	Wrap sprain
Calamine lotion	Cover large cut
Elastic bandage	Cause vomiting
Gauze Bandage	Cover small cut
Iodine	Disinfect cut
Ipecac	Take temperature
Thermometer	Stop itching

Cuts and Scrapes

When you get get a cut or a scrape, the first thing you should do is stop the bleeding. Take a clean paper towel, fold it and press it against the cut. If the cut does not stop bleeding in five minutes, call your doctor immediately. Next, wash the cut with soap and water. Then put a band-aid on the cut to keep it clean.

What should you do when you get a cut or scrape. Fill in the blanks.

1. Stop the _____.

2. Wash with _____.

3. Cover with a _____.

First Aid

Burns

If you get a small burn, place the burn in cold water for a few minutes. Dry gently with a clean towel. Cover loosely with a bandage. Call your parents.

How could you get a small burn?_____

_____

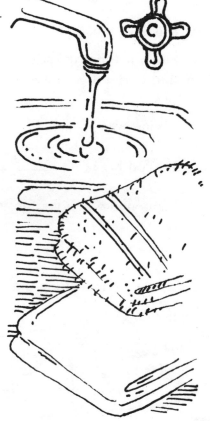

If the burn is large or looks white or charred, call an ambulance right away. While waiting for an ambulance, cover the burn with a clean sheet. If your arms or legs are burned, raise them higher than your heart.

How could you get a serious burn?

_____

_____

_____

Broken Bones

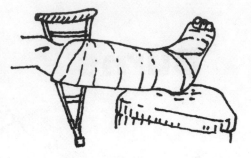

You can not always tell if a bone is broken just by looking at it. It might look the same as it always does and be broken anyway. The important thing to remember is do not move a bone that might be broken. Remove tight clothing around the injury. If you think your foot is broken, take off your shoe. Call for help immediately.

Have you ever a had a broken bone? _____

If yes, answer these questions.
If no, find a friend who has had a broken bone. Ask your friend these questions.

Which bone was broken?_____

How did you break it? _____

What happened when you got to the doctor? _____

_____

How long did it take for the bone to heal?_____

Sprains

You may have a sprain if there is pain, redness, and swelling at a part of your body you have twisted or bumped. A sprained ankle and a sprained wrist are the most common sprains. You can sprain other parts of your body too, such as a knee, a shoulder, or a back.

Here are three rules to follow if you have a sprain.

Rule 1. Do not walk on or move the sprained muscle.

Rule 2. Put ice on the sprain. It will not swell as much.

Rule 3. Wrap the sprain with an elastic bandage.

Here are pictures of some children who have sprained ankles. Which ones are doing the right things?

Animal Bites

You may get scratched or bitten by a dog, a cat, or another animal. First, stop the bleeding with a dry cloth. Then, wash the wound with soap and water. Finally, cover with a bandage. Call your parents. You may need to have a doctor look at the wound immediately.

What should you do to treat an animal bite?

1. Stop the _____.

2. Wash with _____.

3. Cover with a _____.

4. Tell your _____.

Bee Stings

If you get stung by a bee:

Step 1: Scrape out the stinger with a butter knife.

Step 2: Wash with soap and water.

Step 3: Wrap ice in a washcloth and place on sting.

Step 4: If you feel dizzy, sick to your stomach, have trouble breathing, or the sting swells, call a doctor right away.

In what order would you use these four things to treat a bee sting. Number them.

Poisoning

Be careful what you eat and drink. If you or someone who is home with you is poisoned, follow these rules:

Rule 1: Drink two glasses of milk to dilute the poison. Milk will coat the lining of your stomach and reduce burning.

Rule 2: Save the bottle or box that held the poison.

Rule 3: Call Poison Control **immediately**. Find out the number for Poison Control now. This way you will have it if you need it. Post it by the telephone and write it here:_____. If possible, have the bottle in your hand when you call Poison Control. They will want you to read the contents off the label.

Rule 4: If you can not reach poison control, call your doctor.

What is the name of your doctor?_____

What is your doctor's phone number? _____

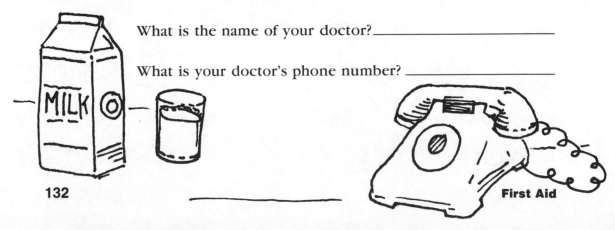

First Aid

Vomiting

It is not unusual to suddenly feel sick and throw up. You might have a stomach virus or have eaten something that disagrees with you. If you do get sick, call your parents.

Lie down and stay quiet. Do not eat or drink anything. You can suck on an ice cube or a lollipop. Place a bucket or large paper bag next to you. This way if you feel sick again, you don't have to run to the bathroom.

Color this picture of a boy who feels sick. He is doing the right things.

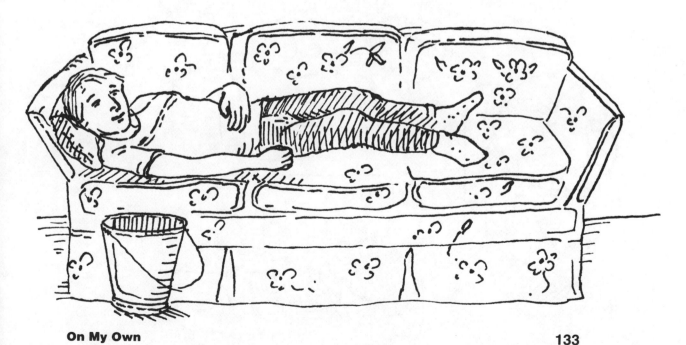

Nosebleed

If you get a nosebleed, sit quietly. Do **not** lie down. Pinch your nose closed for five minutes. Do **not** blow your nose. If you think your nose is broken, or if it doesn't stop bleeding after five minutes, call your parents or a doctor.

Circle the children who are doing the right thing for a nose bleed.

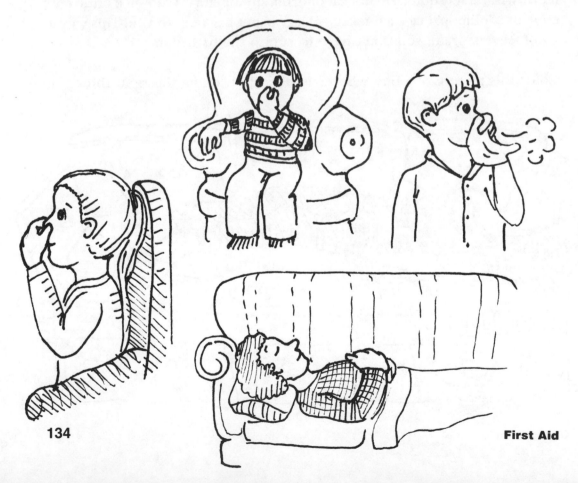

Calling an Ambulance

Y̶ou must remember that you are not a doctor. Do not take any medicine unless a doctor or your parents tell you to. Taking the wrong medicine can be more dangerous than taking no medicine.

Call an ambulance **immediately** if you or one of your brothers and sisters: **has difficulty breathing, has a cut that won't stop bleeding, has swallowed poison, or is in a great deal of pain.**

You can call your parents while you are waiting for the ambulance. Find out the number of an ambulance service near you.

Post it near your phone and write it here. _____

Chapter 10

Emergencies

An emergency is something that happens all of a sudden. When an emergency happens, you have to act right away. There is no time to waste. In a house there are many things that can go wrong. The electricity can go off or a pipe can break. This chapter will teach you what to do if there is an emergency in your house.

Smell Gas

Here are some things you should do if you smell gas. Why should you do these things? Write the reason for each rule.

Rule 1: Call the operator. Ask for **Emergency Gas Service.**

Reason _____

_____

Rule 2: *Do not* light a match.

Reason: _____

_____

Rule 3: *Do not* turn on the oven or stove.

Reason: _____

_____

Rule 4: Open a window.

Reason: _____

_____

Broken Window

Broken windows happen all the time. Name three ways a window can break.

1. _____

2. _____

3. _____

If you get a broken window, follow these rules.

Rule 1. Put your shoes on. **Don't** get glass in your feet.

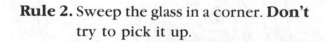

Rule 2. Sweep the glass in a corner. **Don't** try to pick it up.

Rule 3. Tape cardboard or paper over the broken window. Keep the cold air and rain out.

Rule 4. Call your parents. Follow their directions.

Water, Water Everywhere

A flood can happen all of a sudden. A strong rain can cause a basement to flood quickly. If there is a flood in your basement, do not try to fix it. Call your parents and ask them what you should do.

If the faucet starts to leak or a pipe breaks, you should turn off the water. Ask your parents to show you the valve that turns off the water in your house or apartment. Turn the valve to the right to shut off the water.

Here is a picture of a shut off valve. Draw arrows to show which way you would turn it to shut the water off.

Emergencies

Toilet Overflows

If you flush the toilet and it overflows the first thing you should do is shut off the water to the toilet. Look for a wheel or knob by the bottom of the toilet. Turn the knob to the right to shut off the water. Look at the picture. Find the shut-off valve. Notice which way you are supposed to turn it. Now go into your bathroom and find the shut-off valve. If you can't find it, ask your parents to help you.

After you shut the water off, mop up any water on the floor. Now you can try to unplug the toilet. Use a plumber's helper if you have one. Pump up and down a few times until there is very little water left in the bowl. Now you are ready to test if it is fixed. First turn the water back on. Next flush the toilet again. Quickly shut the water off if it looks as if the toilet is going to overflow. Ask your parents for help when they get home.

Lights Out

Most of the time when a light goes out, the light bulb is burned out. If a light goes out, turn the switch off. Put on another light in the room.

When your parents get home, explain the problem to them.

Do **not** try to change the bulb by yourself. Here are three pictures of children trying to change a light bulb. How is each one doing something dangerous?

1. _____

2. _____

3. _____

Emergencies

Electricity Goes Off

Sometimes all the electricity in your house or apartment goes off. All of a sudden, the lights, the television, and anything else that uses electricity will go off. As soon as this happens, the power company tries to fix it. It usually comes back on in a few minutes.

Don't panic. Even when the electricity goes off, the phone still works. Call one of your parents at work. Tell them the problem and ask them what to do. Turn all but one of the switches off. If it is dark out, use a flashlight to help you see. **Never** light candles.

Has the electricity ever gone off in your house? _____

Who was home? _____

What happened? _____

How long did the electricity stay off? _____

Broken Appliances

If an appliance breaks when you are using it, turn it off immediately and unplug it. Do **not** use it again until it is fixed. **Never** touch any electrical object if your hands are wet or you are standing in water.

Make a list of the appliances in your house that you are allowed to use.

_____

_____

_____

_____

_____

Weather Emergencies

There are many types of weather emergencies. Depending on where you live, you might find yourself alone during a thunderstorm, tornado, hurricane, or snowstorm.

Here is a list of weather emergencies. Ask your parents or teacher which ones occur where you live.

_____Thunderstorms

_____Hail Storms

_____Flash Floods

_____Tornadoes

_____Hurricanes

_____Snow Storms

_____Tsunamis

During most weather emergencies, you should stay inside and stay away from the windows. Find out what you should do for each emergency you checked.

Thermostat

You use a thermostat to raise or lower the temperature in your house. Thermostats have two parts. One part is the thermometer. It tells you the temperature in your house. The second part tells the furnace what temperature you would like the house to be.

Here are pictures of two kinds of thermostats. Ask your parents if you have a thermostat in your house. If you do, draw it here and ask them how to use it.

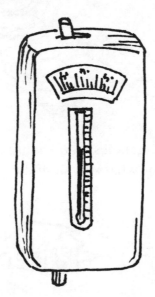

Emergency Kit

Be sure to have an emergency kit in your house so that you are prepared to handle some of these emergencies. Match the things in this emergency kit with why you need them.

Flashlight

Fire Extinguisher

Transistor Radio

First Aid Kit

Water

Food (Non-cook)

Extra Batteries

Put out small fires

Listen to news about weather emergencies

When lights go out

To eat

In case of injury

For flashlight

For cooking and drinking

Chapter 11

Friends

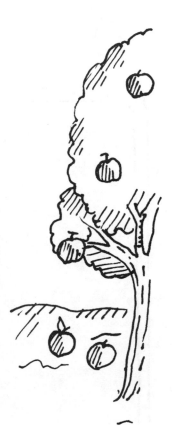

A friend is someone you like spending time with. All friends are different. Some friends are older than you. Other friends are younger than you. Each friend is special. Not all friends like to do the same types of things. You can do different things with different friends. Some things you can do by yourself. But friends can keep you company when you feel like playing with someone. Friends can also help when you feel scared or lonely.

My Friends

Who are your friends? Take this book to school. Have your friends write their names on this page. They can also write little messages to you.

Portraits

Here are two empty picture frames. Draw your picture in one of them. Draw a picture of your best friend in the other one. Write your names under your pictures.

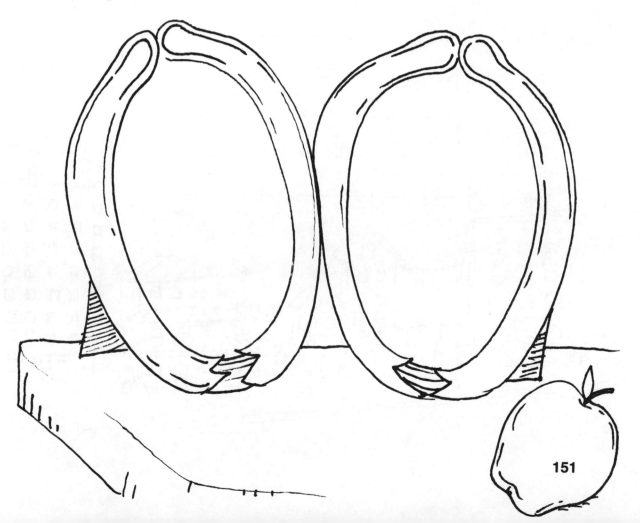

Visiting

Some friends live nearby. Others live far away. Make a list of friends that live close enough that you could walk to their houses.

_____

_____

_____

_____

_____

Rules When Visiting

When visiting friends at their houses after school, follow these rules. Write the reason for each rule after you read it.

Rule 1. Ask your parents if you can go.

Reason: _____

Rule 2. Ask your friend's parents if you may visit.

Reason: _____

Rule 3. Clean up any mess you make.

Reason: _____

Rule 4. Follow the house rules.

Reason: _____

Rule 5. Do **not** walk home when it is dark.

Reason: _____

Friends In?

Some parents let their children have friends in when the children are home alone. Others do not.

What are a few reasons some parents do not want their children to have friends in when they are home alone.

_____

_____

_____

_____

What are a few reasons some parents might let their children have friends in when they are home alone?

_____

_____

_____

_____

Playing with Friends

Spending the afternoon with a friend will make the time you are alone seem shorter. There are a lot of things you can do with a friend that you can not do alone. Make a list of things you can do with a friend that you can not do alone.

_____

_____

_____

_____

_____

Rules to Follow

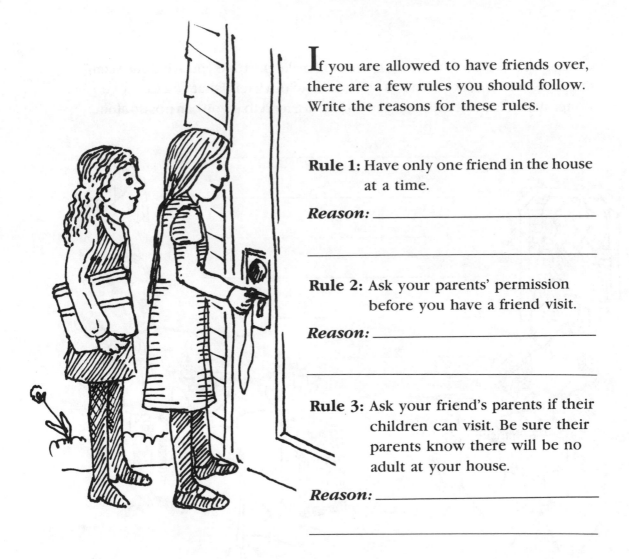

If you are allowed to have friends over, there are a few rules you should follow. Write the reasons for these rules.

Rule 1: Have only one friend in the house at a time.

Reason: _____

_____

Rule 2: Ask your parents' permission before you have a friend visit.

Reason: _____

_____

Rule 3: Ask your friend's parents if their children can visit. Be sure their parents know there will be no adult at your house.

Reason: _____

_____

When your Friends Break the Rules

Sometimes when friends are at your house, they do things you know are wrong. Maybe they are playing with matches or teasing your dog. What should you do?

Here are some things you can do if one of your friends breaks the rules. Which would you do first? Second? Number these steps in the order you would do them. Discuss your answers with your parents.

_____Get a neighbor to come help you.

_____Call your parents.

_____Tell your friend to stop.

_____Call your friend's parents.

_____Ask your friend to leave your house.

Be smart.
Don't ask that friend to visit you again.

The List

Having a friend visit when you are home alone is not the same as having a friend visit when your parents are home. Since no adult is home, you have to pick friends who will follow the rules.

Make a list of friends who would be good guests. Talk with your parents about the children on the list.

_____   _____

_____   _____

_____

Not on the List

There will be some friends that your parents will not want you to have over when they are not home. They are not on the list of friends that are OK to have in the house when your parents are not home.

What would you say in the following situations?

You are home alone. A friend that you are not allowed to have in the house calls you up. That friend wants to know if he or she can come over.

_____

_____

You are home alone. A friend you can not have in the house knocks on your door. He or she wants to come in and play for a few minutes. That friend promises to leave before your parents get home.

_____

_____

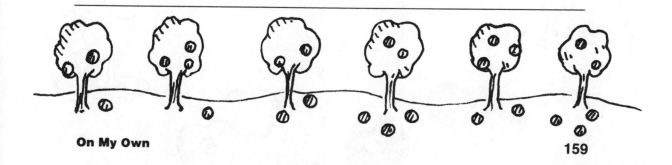

Sharing

Sharing is caring. When you share your food, toys, and time with a friend, you are telling them you care about them. Sharing makes people feel special.

What are some things you share with your friends?

_____

_____

_____

_____

Are there some things you do not want to share with your friends? What are they?

_____

_____

_____

Fighting

Fighting never solves anything. If you and a friend can't agree, talk about it. Don't start yelling, hitting, or kicking. You will only get madder and someone might get hurt. If you can't solve the problem, spend some time away from each other. When you get back together, you both might have some new ideas.

Have you ever had a fight with a friend? _____

What happened? _____

_____

How did you feel after the fight? _____

How did you make up? _____

_____

What could you have done so you would not have had a fight?

_____

Chapter 12

Ready Or Not

Congratulations. You have completed *On My Own*. Are you ready to care for yourself for a little while each day? Can you handle the emergencies that might happen while you are alone?

Here are some true stories of things that happened to other children while they were home alone. What would you do if the same thing happened to you? Talk over your answers with your parents. The answers are on pages 174 and 175.

Ready Or Not

1. One day while Seth is walking home, it starts to rain. He still has six blocks to walk when a car pulls up next to him and stops. The woman who is driving the car rolls down the window. She asks Seth if he wants a ride. Seth has never seen the woman before. But he is cold and it is raining hard. What would you do if you were Seth?

A. Get in the car.

B. Explain you cannot ride with strangers.

C. Keep walking.

D. Wait under a tree for shelter.

Ready Or Not

2. Linda stays home every afternoon with her older brother Robert. They have to stay in until their mother comes home at five-thirty. When their mother comes home, they can go out and play with their friends. Sometimes when they come home from school, Robert goes out to play anyway. Linda is home alone. Linda is scared being home alone. Robert says if she tells on him he will beat her up. What would you do if you were Linda?

A. Go out and play with your friends.

B. Stay in and don't tell on Robert.

C. Call a parent at work and explain you are alone.

D. Tell Robert if he leaves you alone again, you will tell on him.

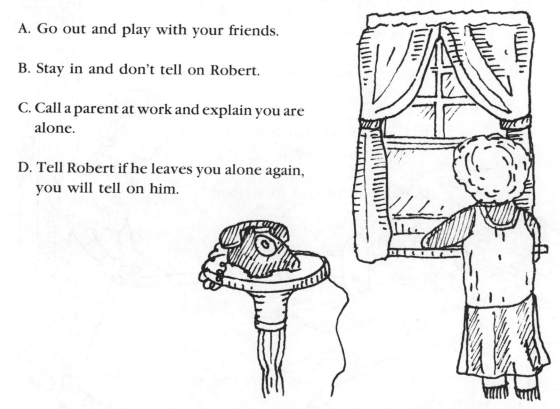

Ready Or Not

3. While walking down the hallway toward her apartment, Karen notices the front door is open. Karen's mother is usually at work when she gets home from school. But Karen is hoping maybe she got home early today. She runs toward the door yelling, "Mom is that you?" No one answers When she gets inside, she notices the whole apartment is a mess. What would you do if you were Karen?

A. Go to a neighbor's to use the phone.

B. Clean up and wait for your parents to get home.

C. Look around your house to see if anything is missing.

D. Call your parents from home.

Ready Or Not

4. Mike rides the bus home from school. He comes inside and takes off his coat. Then he put his books and key on the kitchen table and sits down to watch his favorite television program. Bored while watching, he looks out the window to see Gordon outside on a new bike. He runs outside to take a peek. When he does, the door to his house slams shut. Mike is locked outside. What would you do if you were Mike?

A. Play with Gordon until one of your parents comes home.

B. Call your parents from Gordon's house.

C. Break a window to get inside.

D. Wait at a neighbor's house.

Ready Or Not

5. Sarah is home alone. There is a knock at the door. She asks, "Who is it?"
A strange voice answers, "Is your mother home?" Sarah answers, "My
mother's busy, who is it?" The strange voice says, "I need to use the phone.
My car is out of gas." What would you do if you were Sarah?

A. Let the person in to use the telephone.

B. Call a parent ask what you should do.

C. Tell the person you're sorry, but no one
is allowed to use the phone.

D. Call the police.

168

Ready Or Not

6. Noah is alone before school every morning. He has to get dressed and eat breakfast alone. Today he is running late. Just as he opens the door, he sees the school bus pulling away. What would you do if you were Noah?

A. Go back to bed.

B. Watch television.

C. Call your mother or father at work.

D. Walk to school.

Ready Or Not

7. Markie is home alone one evening while his mother is at work. It is dark outside. Suddenly, a terrible thunderstorm starts. The lights go out and the T.V. goes off. Markie is scared. His mother won't be home for almost two hours. What would you do if you were Markie?

A. Run to a neighbors.

B. Light some candles.

C. Find a flashlight and call a parent on the phone.

D. Hide in your bedroom until your mother comes home.

Ready Or Not

8. Adam walks home from school with his older sister Laura everyday. He is waiting by a telephone pole in front of the school to meet Laura. Twenty minutes have gone by. Laura is still not there. Laura gets out of school the same time as Adam. Laura usually picks him up Adam right away. What would you do if you were Adam?

A. Walk home without your sister.

B. Wait longer.

C. Go back in the school and look for your sister.

D. Call your mom and ask her what to do.

Ready Or Not

9. Julie is home alone. The phone rings. When she answers it a strange man begins talking. He tells her that he loves her and a lot of other weird things. She hangs up the phone right away. One minute later the phone rings again. What would you do if you were Julie?

A. Answer the phone and see who it is.

B. Don't answer the phone anymore that day.

C. Wait until the phone stops ringing and call a parent for advice.

D. Take the phone off the hook so you can't get anymore calls.

Ready Or Not

10. Cindy is home alone watching television. She thinks she smells something burning. She walks from room to room to check for smoke or fire, but finds nothing. Cindy starts watching cartoons again when all of a sudden the wall of the living room is in flames. What would you do if you were Cindy?

A. Call your mom and ask her what to do.

B. Carry your toys and other valuables outside.

C. Call the fire department from your house.

D. Run to a neighbor's or friend's and call the fire department.

Ready Or Not

Check Your Answers. Discuss the stories with your parents.

1. **Keep walking. Don't** get in the car with or talk to strangers.

2. **Call a parent at work and explain you are alone.** Don't be afraid of your older brothers and sisters. Always tell your parents what is happening.

3. **Go to a neighbors to use the phone. <u>Never</u>** enter your house or apartment if a door or window is open or broken.

4. **Call your parent's from Gordon's house.** If you get locked out call your parents, tell them where you are and ask them what to do.

5. **Tell the person you're sorry but no one can use the phone. <u>Never</u>** let anyone in your house you don't know even if it sounds like that person has a good reason.

6. **Call your mother at work.** If you miss the bus or are late getting ready for school, call your parents and tell them the situation. They will tell you what to do.

7. **Find a flashlight and call a parent on the phone.** If the electricity goes out, don't light candles. It's too easy to start a fire. Use a flashlight instead. Most of the time when the power goes out, the phone still works. Use it to get help.

8. **Call your mom and ask her what to do.** The best place to call from is inside the school. Ask your teacher or the school secretary for help. Don't walk home alone without checking with parents.

9. **Wait until the phone stops ringing and call a parent for advice.** Do not take the phone off the hook or stop answering it without asking your parents first. They may be trying to reach you.

10. **Run to a neighbor's or friend's and call the fire department. <u>Never</u>** stay in a house or apartment that is on fire.

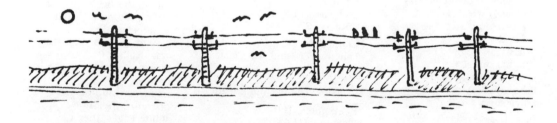

How Did You Do?

9-10 Right....Super
7-8 Right....Good
6 Or Less Right...Read *On My Own* Again

Index